Courage Under Fire
Testing Epictetus's Doctrines in a Laboratory of Human Behavior

James Bond Stockdale

Hoover Institution on War, Revolution and Peace

Stanford University

1993

www.hoover.org

Hoover Essays No. 6

First printing, 1993
Manufactured in the United States of America

24 23   20 19 18 17

Library of Congress Cataloging-in-Publication Data
Stockdale, James B.
        Courage under fire : testing Epictetus's doctrines in a laboratory
of human behavior / James Bond Stockdale.

        p. cm. — (Hoover essays no. 6)
        ISBN-13: 978-0-8179-3692-1 (pbk.: alk. paper)
        ISBN-10: 0-8179-3692-0 (pbk.: alk. paper)
        1. Vietnamese Conflict, 1961–1975—Prisoners and prisons, North
Vietnamese.   2. Vietnamese Conflict, 1961–1975—Personal narratives,
American.   3. Stockdale, James B.   4. Epictetus.   5. Prisoners
of war—United States—Biography.   6. Prisoners of war—Vietnam—
Biography.   I. Title.   II. Series: Hoover essays (Stanford, Calif.: 1992);
no. 6.
DS559.4.S74   1993
959.704'37—dc20
                                                                    93-42455
                                                                        CIP

COURAGE UNDER FIRE
Testing Epictetus's Doctrines in
a Laboratory of Human Behavior

James Bond Stockdale

I came to the philosophic life as a thirty-eight-year-old naval pilot in grad school at Stanford University. I had been in the navy for twenty years and scarcely ever out of a cockpit. In 1962, I began my second year of studying international relations so I could become a strategic planner in the Pentagon. But my heart wasn't in it. I had yet to be inspired at Stanford and saw myself as just processing tedious material about how nations organized and governed themselves. I was too old for that. I knew how political systems operated; I had been beating systems for years.

Then, in what we call a "feel out pass" in stunt flying, I cruised into Stanford's philosophy corner one winter morning. I was gray-haired and in civilian clothes. A voice boomed out of an office, "Can I help you?" The speaker was Philip Rhinelander, dean of Humanities and Sciences, who taught Philosophy 6: The Problems of Good and Evil.

At first he thought I was a professor, but we soon found common ground in the navy because he'd served in World War II. Within fifteen minutes we'd agreed that I would enter his two-term course in the middle, and to make up for my lack of background, I would meet him for an hour a week for a private tutorial in the study of his campus home.

Speech delivered at the Great Hall, King's College, London, Monday, November 15, 1993.

Phil Rhinelander opened my eyes. In that study it all happened for me—my inspiration, my dedication to the philosophic life. From then on, I was out of international relations—I already had enough credits for the master's—and into philosophy. We went from Job to Socrates to Aristotle to Descartes. And then on to Kant, Hume, Dostoyevsky, Camus. All the while, Rhinelander was psyching me out, trying to figure out what I was seeking. He thought my interest in Hume's *Dialogues Concerning Natural Religion* was quite interesting. On my last session, he reached high in his wall of books and brought down a copy of *The Enchiridion*. He said, "I think you'll be interested in this."

Enchiridion means "ready at hand." In other words, it's a hand book. Rhinelander explained that its author, Epictetus, was a very unusual man of intelligence and sensitivity, who gleaned wisdom rather than bitterness from his early firsthand exposure to extreme cruelty and firsthand observations of the abuse of power and self-indulgent debauchery.

Epictetus was born a slave in about A.D. 50 and grew up in Asia Minor speaking the Greek language of his slave mother. At the age of fifteen or so, he was loaded off to Rome in chains in a slave caravan. He was treated savagely for months while en route. He went on the Rome auction block as a permanent cripple, his knee having been shattered and left untreated. He was "bought cheap" by a freedman named Epaphroditus, a secretary to Emperor Nero. He was taken to live at the Nero White House at a time when the emperor was neglecting the empire as he frequently toured Greece as actor, musician, and chariot race driver. When home in Rome in his personal quarters, Nero was busy having his half-brother killed, his wife killed, his mother killed, his second wife killed. Finally, it was Epictetus's master Epaphroditus who cut Nero's throat when he fumbled his own suicide as the soldiers were breaking down his door to arrest him.

That put Epaphroditus under a cloud, and, fortuitously, the now cagey slave Epictetus realized he had the run of Rome. And being a serious and doubtless disgusted young man, he gravitated to the high-minded public lectures of the Stoic teachers who *were* the philosophers of Rome in those days. Epictetus eventually became apprenticed to the very best Stoic teacher in the empire, Musonius

Rufus, and, after ten or more years of study, achieved the status of philosopher in his own right. With that came true freedom in Rome, and the preciousness of that was duly celebrated by the former slave. Scholars have calculated that in his works individual freedom is praised six times more frequently than it is in the New Testament. The Stoics held that all human beings were equal in the eyes of God: male/female, black/white, slave and free.

I read every one of Epictetus's extant writings twice, through two translators. Even with the most conservative translators, Epictetus comes across speaking like a modern person. It is "living speech," not the literary Attic Greek we're used to in men of that tongue. *The Enchiridion* was actually penned not by Epictetus, who was above all else a determined teacher and man of modesty who would never take the time to transcribe his own lectures, but by one of his most meticulous and determined students. The student's name was Arrian, a very smart, aristocratic Greek in his twenties. After hearing his first few lectures, he is reported to have exclaimed something like, "Son of a gun! We've got to get this guy down on parchment!"

With Epictetus's consent, Arrian took down his words verbatim in some kind of frantic shorthand he devised. He bound the lectures into books; in the two years he was enrolled in Epictetus's school, he filled eight books. Four of them disappeared sometime before the Middle Ages. It was then that the remaining four got bound together under the title *Discourses of Epictetus*. Arrian put *The Enchiridion* together after he had finished the eight. It is just highlights from them "for the busy man." Rhinelander told me that last morning, "As a military man, I think you'll have a special interest in this. Frederick the Great never went on a campaign without a copy of this handbook in his kit."

I'll never forget that day, and the essence of what that great man had to say as we said good-bye was burned into my brain, It went very much like this: Stoicism is a noble philosophy that proved more praticable than a modern cynic would expect. The Stoic viewpoint is often misunderstood because the casual reader misses the point that all talk is in reference to the "inner life" of man. Stoics belittle physical harm, but this is not braggadocio. They are speaking of it in comparison to the devastating agony of shame they fancied good men generating when they knew in their hearts that they had *failed* to do their duty vis-à-vis their fellow men or God. Although pagan, the Stoics had a monotheistic, *natural* religion and were great contributors to Christian thought. The fatherhood of God and the brotherhood of man were Stoic concepts before Christianity. In fact, one of their early theoreticians, named Chrysippus, made the analogy of what might be called the *soul* of the universe to the *breath* of a human, *pneuma* in Greek. This Stoic conception of a celestial pneuma is said to be the great-grandfather of the Christian Holy Ghost. Saint Paul, a Hellenized Jew brought up in Tarsus, a Stoic town in Asia Minor, always used the Greek word *pneuma*, or breath, for "soul."

Rhinelander told me that the Stoic demand for disciplined thought naturally won only a small minority to its standard, but that those few were everywhere the best. Like its Christian counterparts, Calvinism and Puritanism, it produced the strongest characters of its time. In theory, a doctrine of pitiless perfection, it actually created men of courage, saintliness, and goodwill. Rhinelander singled out three examples: Cato the Younger, Emperor Marcus Aurelius, and Epictetus. Cato was the great Roman republican who pitted himself against Julius Caesar. He was the unmistakable hero of George Washington; scholars find quotations of this man in Washington's farewell address—without quotation marks. Emperor Marcus Aurelius took the Roman Empire to the pinnacle of its power and influence. And Epictetus, the great teacher, played his part in changing the leadership of Rome from the swill he had known in the Nero White House to the power and decency it knew under Marcus Aurelius.

Marcus Aurelius was the last of the five emperors (all with Stoic connections) who successively ruled throughout that period Edward Gibbon described in his *Decline and Fall of the Roman Empire* as follows: "If a man were called upon to fix the period in the history of the world during which the condition of the human race was most happy and prosperous, he would without hesitation name that which elapsed from the accession of Nerva (A.D. 96) to the death of Marcus Aurelius (A.D. 180). The united reigns of the five emperors of the era are possibly the only period of history in which the happiness of a great people was the sole object of government."

Epictetus drew the same sort of audience Socrates had drawn five hundred years earlier—young aristocrats destined for careers in finance, the arts, public service. The best families sent him their best sons in their middle twenties—to be told what the good life consisted of, to be disabused of the idea that they deserved to become playboys, the point made clear that their job was to serve their fellow men.

In his inimitable, frank language, Epictetus explained that his curriculum was *not* about "revenues or income, or peace or war, but about happiness and unhappiness, success and failure, slavery and freedom." His model graduate was not a person "able to speak fluently about philosophic principles as an idle babbler, but about things that will do you good if your child dies, or your brother dies, or if you must die or be tortured." "Let others practice lawsuits, others study problems, others syllogisms; here you practice how to die, how to be enchained, how to be racked, how to be exiled." A man is responsible for his own "judgments, even in dreams, in drunkenness, and in melancholy madness." Each individual brings about his own good and his own evil, his good fortune, his ill fortune, his happiness, and his wretchedness. And to top all this off, he held that it is *unthinkable* that one man's error could cause another's suffering. Suffering, like everything else in Stoicism, was *all down here*—remorse at destroying *yourself*.

So what Epictetus was telling his students was that there can be no such thing as being the "victim" of another. You can only be a "victim" of *yourself*. It's all in how you discipline your mind. Who is your master? "He who has authority over *any* of the things on which you have set your heart." "What is the result at which all virtue aims? *Serenity*." "Show me a man who though sick is happy, who though in danger is happy, who though in prison is happy, and I'll show you a Stoic."

When I got my degree, Sybil and I packed up our four sons and family belongings and headed to Southern California. I was to take command of Fighter Squadron 51, flying supersonic F-8 Crusaders, first at the Miramar Naval Air Station, near San Diego, and later, of course, at sea aboard various aircraft carriers in the western Pacific. Exactly three years after we drove up to our new home near San Diego, I was shot down and captured in North Vietnam.

During those three years, I had launched on three seven-month cruises to the waters off Vietnam. On the first we were occupied with general surveillance of the fighting erupting in the South; on the second I led the first-ever American bombing raid against North Vietnam; and on the third, I was flying in combat almost daily as the air wing commander of the USS *Oriskany*. But on my bedside table, no matter what carrier I was aboard, were my Epictetus books: *Enchiridion*, *Discourses*, Xenophon's *Memorabilia* of Socrates, and *The Iliad* and *The Odyssey*. (Epictetus expected his students to be familiar with Homer's plots.) I didn't have time to be a bookworm, but I spent several hours each week buried in them.

I think it was obvious to my close friends, and certainly to me, that I was a changed man and, I have to say, a better man for my introduction to philosophy and especially to Epictetus. I was on a different track—certainly not an antimilitary track but to some extent an antiorganization track. Against the backdrop of all the posturing and fumbling around peacetime military organizations seem to have to go through, to accept the need for graceful and unself-conscious improvisation under pressure, to break away from set procedures forces you to be reflective, reflective as you put a new mode of operation together. I had become a man detached—not aloof but detached—able to throw out the book without the slightest hesitation when it no longer matched the external circumstances. I was able to put juniors over seniors without embarrassment when their wartime instincts were more reliable. This new abandon, this new built-in flexibility I had gained, was to pay off later in prison.

But undergirding my new confidence was the realization that I had found the proper philosophy for the military arts as I practiced them. The Roman Stoics coined the formula *Vivere militare!*—"Life is being a soldier." Epictetus in *Discourses*: "Do you not know that life is a soldier's service? One must keep guard, another go out to reconnoitre, another take the field. If you neglect your responsibilities when some severe order is laid upon you, do you not understand to what a pitiful state you bring the army in so far as in you lies?" *Enchiridion*: "Remember, you are an actor in a drama of such sort as the Author chooses—if short, then in a short one; if long, then in a long one. If it be his pleasure that you should enact a poor man, or a cripple, or a ruler, see that you act it well. For this is your business—to act well the given part, but to choose it belongs to Another." "Every one of us, slave or free, has come into this world with *innate* conceptions as to good and bad, noble and shameful, becoming and unbecoming, happiness and unhappiness, *fitting and inappropriate*." "If you regard yourself as a man and as a part of some whole, it is fitting for you now to be sick and now to make a voyage and run risks, and now to be in want, and on occasion to die before your time. Why, then are you vexed? Would you have someone else be sick of a fever now, someone else go on a voyage, someone else die? For it is impossible in such a body as ours, that is, in this universe that envelops us, among these fellow-creatures of ours, that such things should not happen, some to one man, some to another."

On September 9, 1965, I flew at 500 knots right into a flak trap, at tree-top level, in a little A-4 airplane—the cockpit walls not even three feet apart—which I couldn't steer after it was on fire, its control system shot out. After ejection I had about thirty seconds to make my last statement in freedom before I landed in the main street of a little village right ahead. And so help me, I whispered to myself: "Five years down there, at least. I'm leaving the world of technology and entering the world of Epictetus."

"Ready at hand" from *The Enchiridion* as I ejected from that airplane was the understanding that a Stoic always kept *separate* files in his mind for (A) those things that are "up to him" and (B) those things that are "not up to him." Another way of saying it is (A) those things that are "within his power" and (B) those things that are "beyond his power." Still another way of saying it is (A) those things that are within the grasp of "his Will, his Free Will" and (B) those things that are beyond it. All in category B are "external," beyond my control, ultimately dooming me to fear and anxiety if I covet them. All in category A are up to me, within my power, within my will, and properly subjects for my total concern and involvement. They include my opinions, my aims, my aversions, my own grief, my own joy, my judgments, my attitude about what is going on, my own good, and my own evil.

To explain why "your own good and your own evil" is on that list, I want to quote Alexander Solzhenitsyn from his Gulag book. He writes about that point in prison when he realizes the strength of his residual powers, and starts what I called to myself "gaining moral leverage"; riding the updrafts of occasional euphoria as you realize you are getting to know yourself and the world for the first time. He calls it "ascending" and names the chapter in which this appears "The Ascent":

> It was only when I lay there on the rotting prison straw that I sensed within myself the first stirrings of *good*. Gradually it was disclosed to me that the line separating good and evil passes not between states nor between classes nor between political parties, but right through every human heart, through all human hearts. And that is why I turn back to the years of my imprisonment and say, sometimes to the astonishment of those about me, "Bless you, prison, for having been a part of my life."

I came to understand that long before I read it. Solzhenitsyn learned, as I and others have learned, that good and evil are not just abstractions you kick around and give lectures about and attribute to this person and that. The only good and evil that means anything is right in your own heart, within your will, within your power, where it's up to you. *Enchiridion 32*: "Things that are not within our own power, not without our Will, can by no means be either good or evil." *Discourses*: "Evil lies in the evil use of moral purpose, and good the opposite. The course of the Will determines good or bad fortune, and one's balance of misery and happiness." In short, what the Stoics say is "Work with what you have control of and you'll have your hands full."

What is not up to you? beyond your power? not subject to your will in the last analysis? For starters, let's take "your station in life." As I glide down toward that little town on my short parachute ride, I'm just about to learn how negligible is my control over my station in life. It's not at all up to me. I'm going right now from being the leader of a hundred-plus pilots and a thousand men and, goodness knows, all sorts of symbolic status and goodwill, to being *an object of contempt*. I'll be known as a "criminal." But that's not *half* the revelation that is the realization of your own *fragility*—that you can be reduced by wind and rain and ice and seawater or *men* to a helpless, sobbing wreck—unable to control even your own bowels—

in a matter of *minutes*. And, more than even that, you're going to face
fragilities you never before let yourself believe you could have—like
after mere minutes, in a flurry of action while being bound with
tourniquet-tight ropes, with care, by a professional, hands behind,
jackknifed forward and down toward your ankles held secure in lugs
attached to an iron bar, that, with the onrush of anxiety, knowing
your upper body's circulation has been stopped and feeling the ever-
growing induced pain and the ever-closing-in of claustrophobia, you
can be made to blurt out answers, sometimes correct answers, to
questions about anything they know you know. (Hereafter, I'll just
call that situation "taking the ropes.")

"Station in life," then, can be changed from that of a dignified
and competent gentleman of culture to that of a panic-stricken,
sobbing, self-loathing wreck in a matter of minutes. So what? To
live under the false pretense that you will forever have control of
your station in life is to ride for a fall; you're asking for disappoint-
ment. So make sure in your heart of hearts, in your inner self, that
you treat your station in life with *indifference*, not with contempt,
only with *indifference*.

And so also with a long long list of things that some unreflective
people assume they're assured of controlling to the last instance:
your body, property, wealth, health, life, death, pleasure, pain,
reputation. Consider "reputation," for example. Do what you will,
reputation is at least as fickle as your station in life. *Others* decide
what your reputation is. Try to make it as good as possible, but don't
get hooked on it. Don't be ravenous for it and start chasing it in
tighter and tighter circles. As Epictetus says, "For what are tragedies
but the portrayal in tragic verse of the sufferings of men who have
admired things external?" In your heart of hearts, when you get out
the key and open up that old rolltop desk where you really keep
your stuff, don't let "reputation" get mixed up with your *moral
purpose* or your *will power*; they *are* important. Make sure "reputation" is in that box in the bottom drawer marked "matters of indifference." As Epictetus says, "He who craves or shuns things not
under his control can neither be faithful nor free, but must himself
be changed and tossed to and fro and must end by subordinating
himself to others."

I know the difficulties of gulping this down right away. You keep thinking of practical problems. Everybody has to play the game of life. You can't just walk around saying, "I don't give a damn about health or wealth or whether I'm sent to prison or not." Epictetus took time to explain better what he meant. He says everybody should play the game of life—that the best play it with "skill, form, speed, and grace." But, like most games, you play it with a ball. Your team devotes all its energies to getting the ball across the line. But after the game, what do you do with the ball? Nobody much cares. It's not worth anything. The competition, the game, was the thing. The ball was "used" to make the game possible, but it in itself is not of any value that would justify falling on your sword for it.

Once the game is over, the ball is properly a matter of indifference. Epictetus on another occasion used the example of shooting dice—the dice being matters of indifference, once their numbers had turned up. To exercise *judgment* about whether to accept the numbers or roll again is a *willful* act, and thus *not* a matter of indifference. Epictetus's point is that our *use* of externals is not a matter of indifference because our actions are products of our will and we totally control that, but that the dice themselves, like the ball, are material over which we have no control. They are externals that we cannot afford to covet or be earnest about, else we might set our hearts on them and become slaves of such others as control them.

These explanations of this concept seem so modern, yet I have just given you practically verbatim quotes of Epictetus's remarks to his students in Nicopolis, colonial Greece, two thousand years ago.

So I took those core thoughts into prison; I also remembered a lot of attitude-shaping remarks. Here's Epictetus on how to stay off the hook: "A man's master is he who is able to confer or remove whatever that man seeks or shuns. Whoever then would be free, let him wish nothing, let him decline nothing, which depends on others; else he must necessarily be a slave." And here's why never to beg: "For it is better to die of hunger, exempt from fear and guilt, than to live in affluence with perturbation." Begging sets up a demand for quid pro quos, deals, agreements, reprisals, the pits.

If you want to protect yourself from "fear and guilt," and those are the crucial pincers, the real long-term destroyers of will, you have to get rid of all your instincts to compromise, to meet people halfway. You have to learn to stand aloof, never give openings for deals, never level with your adversaries. You have to become what Ivan Denisovich called a "slow movin' cagey prisoner."

All that, over the previous three years, I had *unknowingly* put away for the future. So, to return to my bailing out of my A-4, I can hear the noontime shouting and pistol shots and whining bullets ripping my parachute canopy and see the fists waving in the street below as my chute hooks a tree but deposits me on the ground in good shape. With two quick-release fastener flips, I'm free of the parachute, and immediately gang tackled by the ten or fifteen town roughnecks I had seen in my peripheral vision, pounding up the road from my right.

I don't want to exaggerate this or indicate that I was surprised at my reception. It was just that when the gang tackling and pummeling was all over, and it lasted for two or three minutes before a man with a pith helmet got there to blow his police whistle, I had a very badly broken leg that I felt sure would be with me for life. My hunch turned out to be right. Later, I felt some relief—but only minor—from another Epictetus admonition I remembered: "Lameness is an impediment to the leg, but not to the Will; and say this to yourself with regard to everything that happens. For you will find such things to be an impediment to something else, but not truly to yourself."

But during the time interval between pulling the ejection handle and coming to rest on the street, I had become a man with a mission. I can't explain this without unloading a little emotional baggage that was part of my military generation's legacy in 1965.

In the aftermath of the Korean War, just over ten years before, we all had memories of reading about, and seeing early television news accounts of, U.S. government investigations into the behavior of some American prisoners of war in North Korea and mainland China. There was a famous series of articles in the *New Yorker* magazine that later became a book entitled *In Every War but One*. The gist of it was that in prison camps for Americans, it was every man for himself. Since those days, I've come to know officers who were prisoners of war there, and I now see much of that as selective reporting and as a bum rap. However, there were cases of young soldiers who were confused by the times, scared to death, in cold weather, treating each other like dogs fighting over scraps, throwing each other out in the snow to die, and nobody doing anything about it.

This could not go on, and President Eisenhower commissioned the writing of the American Fighting Man's Code of Conduct. It is written in the form of a personal pledge. Article 4: "If I become a prisoner of war, I will keep faith with my fellow prisoners. I will give no information or take part in any action which might be harmful to my comrades. If I am senior, I will take command. If not, I will obey the lawful orders of those appointed over me and will back them up in every way." In other words, as of the moment Eisenhower signed the document, American prisoners of war were never to escape the chain of command; the war goes on behind bars. As an insider, I knew the whole setup—that the North Vietnamese already held about twenty-five prisoners, probably in Hanoi, that I was the only wing commander to survive an ejection, and that I would be their senior, their commanding officer, and would remain so, very likely, throughout this war that I felt sure would last at least another five years. And here I was starting off crippled and flat on my back.

Epictetus turned out to be right. After a very crude operation, I was on crutches within a couple of months, and the crooked leg, healing itself, was strong enough to hold me up without the crutches in about a year. All told, it was only a temporary setback from things that were important to me, and being cast in the role as the sovereign head of an American expatriate colony that was destined to remain autonomous, out of communication with Washington, for years on end was very important to me. I was forty-two years old—still on crutches, dragging a leg, at considerably less than my normal weight, with hair down near my shoulders, my body unbathed since I had been catapulted from the *Oriskany*, a beard that had not seen a razor since I arrived—when I took command (clandestinely, of course, the North Vietnamese would never acknowledge our rank) of about fifty Americans. That expatriate colony would grow to over four hundred—all officers, all college graduates, all pilots or backseat electronic wizards. I was determined to "play well the given part."

The key word for all of us at first was "fragility." Each of us, before we were ever in shouting distance of another American, was

made to "take the ropes." That was a real shock to our systems—
and, as with all shocks, its impact on our inner selves was a lot more
impressive and lasting and important than to our limbs and torsos.
These were the sessions where we were taken down to submission,
and made to blurt out distasteful confessions of guilt and American
complicity into antique tape recorders, and then to be put in what
I call "cold soak," a month or so of total isolation to "contemplate
our crimes." What we actually contemplated was what even the
most laid-back American saw as his betrayal of himself and everything he stood for. It was there that I learned what "Stoic Harm"
meant. A shoulder broken, a bone in my back broken, a leg broken
twice were *peanuts* by comparison. Epictetus: "Look not for any
greater harm than this: destroying the trustworthy, self-respecting
well-behaved man within you."

When put into a regular cell block, hardly an American came
out of that experience without responding something like this when
first whispered to by a fellow prisoner next door: "You don't want
to talk to me; I am a traitor." And because we were equally fragile,
it seemed to catch on that we all replied something like this: "Listen,
pal, there are no virgins in here. You should have heard the kind of
statement I made. Snap out of it. We're all in this together. What's
your name? Tell me about yourself." To hear that last was, for most
new prisoners just out of initial shakedown and cold soak, a turning
point in their lives.

But the new prisoner's learning process was just beginning. Soon
enough he would realize that things were not at all like some had
told him in survival training—that if you made a good stiff showing
of resistance in the opening chapters, the interrogators would lose
interest in you and you would find yourself merely relegated to
boredom, to "sitting out the war," to "languishing in your cell," as
the uninitiated novelists love to describe the predicament. No, the
war went on behind bars—there was no such thing as the jailers
giving up on you as a hopeless case. Their political beliefs *made*
them believe you could be made to see things their way; it was just
a matter of time. And so you were marched to the interrogation
room endlessly, particularly on the occasions of your being appre-
hended breaking one of the myriad rules that were posted on your
cell wall—"trip wire" rules, which paid dividends for the commissar

if his interrogator could get you to fall prey to his wedge of *shame*. The currency at the game table, where you and the interrogator faced one another in a duel of wits, was *shame*, and I learned that unless he could impose shame on me, or unless I imposed it on myself, he had nothing going for him. (Force was available, but that required the commissar's okay.)

For Epictetus, emotions were acts of will. Fear was not something that came out of the shadows of the night and enveloped you; he charged *you* with the total responsibility of starting it, stopping it, controlling it. This was one of Stoicism's biggest demands on a person. Stoics can be made to sound like lazy brutes when they are described merely as people indifferent to most everything but good and evil, people who make stingy use of emotions like pity and sympathy. But add this requirement of total personal responsibility for each and every one of your emotions, and you're talking about a person with his hands full. I whispered a "chant" to myself as I was marched at gunpoint to my daily interrogation: "control fear, control guilt, control fear, control guilt." And I devised methods of deflecting my gaze to obscure such fear or guilt as doubtless emerged in my eyes when I temporarily lost control under questioning. You could be bashed for failure to look at the face of your interrogator; I concentrated on his left earlobe, and he seemed to get used to it— thought I was a little cockeyed, probably. Controlling your emotions is difficult but can be *empowering*. Epictetus: "For it is *within you*, that both your destruction and deliverance lie." Epictetus: "The judgment seat and a prison is each a place, the one high, the other low; but the *attitude of your will* can be kept the same, if you *want* to keep it the same, in either place."

We organized a clandestine society via our wall tap code—a society with our own laws, traditions, customs, even heroes. To explain how it could be that we would order each other into more torture, order each other to refuse to comply with specific demands, intentionally call the bluff of our jailers and in a real sense force them to repeat the full ropes process to another submission, I'll quote a statement that could have come from at least half of those wonderful competitive fly-boys I found myself locked up with: "We are in a spot like we've never been in before. But we deserve to maintain our self-respect, to have the feeling we are fighting back.

We can't refuse to do every degrading thing they demand of us, but it's up to you, boss, to pick out things we must all refuse to do unless and until they put us through the ropes again. We deserve to sleep at night. We at least deserve to have the satisfaction that we are hewing to our leader's orders. Give us the list; what are we to take torture for?"

I know this sounds like strange logic, but in a sense it was a first step in claiming what was rightfully *ours*. Epictetus said, "The judge will do some things to you which are thought to be terrifying; but how can he *stop you* from taking the punishment *he threatened?*" That's *my* kind of Stoicism. You have a right to make them hurt you, and they don't like to do that. When my fellow prisoner Ev Alvarez, the very first pilot they captured, was released with the rest of us, the prison commissar told him: "You Americans were nothing like the French; we could count on them to be reasonable." Ha!

I put a lot of thought into what those first orders should be. They would be orders that *could be obeyed*, not a "cover your ass" move of reiterating some U.S. government policy like "name, rank, serial number, and date of birth," which had no chance of standing up in the torture room. My mind-set was "we here under the gun are the experts, we are the masters of our fate, ignore guilt-inducing echoes of hollow edicts, throw out the book and write your own." My orders came out as easy-to-remember acronyms. The principal one was BACK US: Don't Bow in public; stay off the Air; admit no Crimes, never Kiss them goodbye. "US" could be interpreted as United States, but it *really* meant "Unity over Self." Loners make out in an enemy's prison, so my first rule of togetherness in there was that each of us had to work at the lowest common denominator, never negotiating for himself but only for *all*.

Prison life became a crazy mixture of an old regime and a new one. The old was the political prison routine, mainly for dissenters and domestic enemies of the state. It was designed and run by old-fashioned Third World Communists of the Ho Chi Minh cut. It revolved around the idea of "repentance" for your "crimes" of anti-social behavior. American prisoners, street criminals, and domestic political enemies of the state were all in the same prison. We never saw a "POW camp" like the movies show. The communist jail was part psychiatric clinic and part reform school. North Vietnam protocol called for making *all* their inmates demonstrate shame—bowing to all guards, heads low, never looking at the sky, frequent sessions with your interrogator if, for no other reason, to check your *attitude* and, if judged "wrong," then maybe down the torture chute of confession of guilt, of apology, and then the inevitable payoff of atonement.

The new regime, superimposed on the above, was for Americans only. It was a propaganda factory, supervised by English-speaking young bureaucratic army officers with quotas to fill, quotas set by the political arm of the government: press interviews with visiting left-wing Americans, propaganda films to shoot (starring intimidated "American air pirates"), and so on.

An encapsulated history of how this bifurcated prison philosophy fared is that the propaganda footage and interviews started to backfire. Smart American college men were salting their acts with sentences with double meanings, gestures read as funny-obscene by Western audiences, and practical jokes. One of my best friends, tortured to give names of pilots he knew who had turned in their wings in opposition to the war, said there were only two: Lieutenants Clark Kent and Ben Casey (then-popular fictional characters in America). That joke was headlined on the front page of the *San Diego Union*, and somebody sent a copy back to the government in Hanoi. As a result of that friendly gesture from a fellow American, Nels Tanner went into three successive days of rope torture, followed by 123 days in leg stocks, all while isolated of course.

So after several of these stunts, which cost the Vietnamese much loss of face, North Vietnam resorted to getting their propaganda only from the relatively *few* (less than 5 percent) of the Americans they could trust *not* to act up: real loners who, for different reasons, never joined the prisoner organization, never wanted to get into the tap code network, well-known sleaze balls we came to call *finks*. The vast majority of my constituents were enraged by their actions and took it upon themselves to diligently memorize data that would convict them in an American court-martial. But when we got home our government ruled against my bringing charges.

The great mass of all other Americans in Hanoi were by all standards "honorable prisoners," but that is not to say there was

anything like a homogeneous prison regime we all shared. People
like to think that because we were all in the Hanoi prison system,
we had all these common experiences. It's not so. These *differing*
regimes became marked when our prison organization stultified the
propaganda efforts of this two-headed monster they called the "Prison
Authority." They turned to vengeance against the leadership of my
organization and to an effort to break down the morale of the others
by baiting them with an amnesty program in which they would
compete for early release by being compliant with North Vietnam's
wishes.

In May 1967, the public address system blared out: "Those of
you who repent, truly repent, will be able to go home before the
war is over. Those few diehards who insist on inciting the other
criminals to oppose the camp authority will be sent to a special dark
place." I immediately put out an order forbidding any American to
accept early release, but that is not to say I was a lone man on a
white horse. I didn't have to sell that one; it was accepted with
obvious relief and spontaneous jubilation by the overwhelming
majority.

Guess who went to the "dark place." They isolated my leadership
team—me and my cohort of ten top men—and sent us into exile.
The Vietnamese worked very hard to learn our habits, and they
knew who were the troublemakers and who were "not making any
waves." They isolated those I trusted most; everybody had a long
record of solitary and rope-mark pedigrees. Not all were seniors; we
had seniors in prison who would not even communicate with the
man next door. One of my ten was only twenty-four years old—
born after I was in the navy. He was a product of my recent shipboard
tendencies: "When instincts and rank are out of phase, take the
guy with the instincts." All of us stayed in solitary throughout,
starting with two years in leg irons in a little high-security prison
right beside North Vietnam's "Pentagon"—their Ministry of De-
fense, a typical old French building. There are chapters upon chapters after that, but what they came down to in my case was a strung-
out vengeance fight between the "Prison Authority" and those of
us who refused to quit trying to be our brothers' keepers. The stakes
grew to *nervous breakdown* proportions. One of the eleven of us died
in that little prison we called Alcatraz, but even including him,

there was not a man who wound up with less than three and a half years of solitary, and four of us had more than four years. To give you a sense of proportion on how the total four hundred fared on solo, one hundred had none, more than half of the other three hundred had less than a year, and half of those with less than a year had less than a month. So the average for the four hundred was considerably less than six months.

Howie Rutledge, one of the four of us with more than four years, went back to school and got a master's degree after we got home, and his thesis concentrated on the question of whether long-term erosion of human purpose was more effectively achieved by torture or isolation. He mailed out questionnaires to us (who had also all taken the ropes at least ten times) and others with records of extreme prison abuse. He found that those who had less than two years' isolation and plenty of torture said torture was the trump card; those with more than two years' isolation and plenty of torture said that for long-term modification of behavior, isolation was the way to go. From my viewpoint, you can get used to repeated rope torture—there are some tricks for minimizing your losses in that game. But keep a man, even a very strong-willed man, in isolation for three or more years, and he starts looking for a friend—*any* friend, regardless of nationality or ideology.

Epictetus once gave a lecture to his faculty complaining about the common tendency of new teachers to slight the stark realism of Stoicism's challenges in favor of giving the students an uplifting, rosy picture of how they could meet the harsh requirements of the good life painlessly. Epictetus said: "Men, the lecture-room of the philosopher is a hospital; students ought not to walk out of it in pleasure, but in pain." If Epictetus's lecture room was a hospital, my prison was a laboratory—a laboratory of human behavior. I chose to test his postulates against the demanding real-life challenges of my laboratory. And as you can tell, I think he passed with flying colors.

It's hard to discuss in public the real-life challenges of that laboratory because people ask all the wrong questions: How was the food? That's always the first one, and in a place like I've been, that's so far down the scale you want to cry. Did they harm you physically? What was the nature of the *device* they used to harm you? Always the device or the truth serum or the electric shock treatment—all of which would totally defeat the purpose of a person seriously trying to break down your will. All those things would give *you* a feeling of moral superiority, which is the last thing he would want to have happen. I'm not talking about brainwashing; there is no such thing. I'm talking about having looked over the brink and seen the bottom of the pit and realized the truth of that linchpin of Stoic thought: that the thing that brings down a man is not *pain* but *shame*!

Why did those men in "cold soak" after their first rope trip eat their hearts out and feel so unworthy when the first American contacted them? Epictetus knew human nature well. In that prison laboratory, I do not know of a single case where a man was able to erase his conscience pangs with some laid-back pop psychology theory of cause and effect. Epictetus emphasizes time and again that a man who lays off the causes of his actions to third parties or forces is not leveling with himself. He must live with his own judgments if he is to be honest with himself. (And the "cold soak" tends to make you honest.) "But if a person subjects me to fear of death, he compels me," says a student. "No," says Epictetus, "It is neither death, nor exile, nor toil, nor any such things that is the cause of your doing, or not doing, *anything*, but only your opinions and the decisions of your Will." "What is the fruit of your doctrines?" someone asked Epictetus. "Tranquility, fearlessness, and freedom," he answered. You can have these only if you are honest and take responsibility for your own actions. You've got to get it *straight!* You are in charge of *you*.

Did I preach these things in prison? Certainly not. You soon learned that if the guy next door was doing okay, that meant that he had all his philosophical ducks lined up in his own way. You soon realized that when you dared to spout high-minded philosophical suggestions through the wall, you always got a very reluctant response.

No, I never tapped or mentioned Stoicism once. But some sharp guys read the signs in my actions. After one of my long isolations outside the cell blocks of the prison, I was brought back into signaling range of the fold, and my point of contact was a man named Dave Hatcher. As was standard operating procedure on a first contact after a long separation, we started off not with gushes of news but with first, an agreed-upon danger signal, second, a cover story for each of us if we were caught, and third, a backup communications system if this link was compromised—"slow movin' cagey prisoner" precautions. Hatcher's backup communication for me was a note drop by an old sink near a place we called the Mint, the isolation cell block of Hatcher's "Las Vegas" wing of the prison— a place he rightly guessed I would soon enough be in. Every day we would signal for fifteen minutes over a wall between his cell block and my "no man's land."

Then I got back into trouble. At that time the commissar of prisons had had me isolated and under almost constant surveillance for the year since I had staged a riot in Alcatraz to get us out of leg irons. I was barred from all prisoner cell blocks. I had special handlers, and they caught me with an outbound note that gave leads I knew the interrogators could develop through torture. The result would be to implicate my friends in "black activities" (as the North Vietnamese called them). I had been through those ropes more than a dozen times, and I knew I could *contain* material—*so long as they didn't know I knew it.* But this note would open doors that could lead to more people getting killed in there. We had lost a few in big purges—I think in torture overshoots—and I was getting tired of it. It was the fall of 1969, and I had been in this role for four years and saw nothing left for me to do but check out. I was solo in the main torture room in an isolated part of the prison, the night before what they told me would be my day to spill my guts. There was an eerie mood in the prison. Ho Chi Minh had just died, and his special dirge music was in the air. I was to sit up all night in traveling irons. My chair was near the only paned glass window in the prison. I was able to waddle over and break the window stealthily. I went after my wrist arteries with the big shards. I had knocked the light out, but the patrol guard happened to find me passed out in a pool of blood but still breathing. The Vietnamese sounded the alert, got their doctor, and saved me.

Why? It was not until after I was released years later that I learned that that very week, Sybil had been in Paris demanding humane treatment for prisoners. She was on world news, a public figure, and the last thing the North Vietnamese needed was me dead. There had been a very solemn crowd of senior North Vietnamese officers in that room as I was revived.

Prison torture, *as we had known it in Hanoi*, ended for everybody that night.

Of course it was months before we could be sure that was so. All I knew at the time was that in the morning, after my arms had been dressed and bandaged, the commissar himself brought in a hot cup of sweet tea, told my surveillance guard to take off my leg irons, and asked me to sit at the table with him. "Why did you do this, Sto-dale? You know I sit with the army's General Staff; they've asked for a full report this morning." (It was not unusual for us to talk like that by that time.) But he never once mentioned the note, nor did anybody else thereafter. *That* was unprecedented. After a couple of months in a tiny isolated cell we called Calcutta to let my arms heal, they blindfolded me and walked me right into the Las Vegas cell block. The isolation and special surveillance were over. I was put solo, of course, in the Mint.

Dave Hatcher knew I was back because I was walked under his window, and though he could not peek out, he could listen and over the years had attuned his ear to my walking "signature," my limping gait. Soon enough, the rusty wire over the sink in the washroom was bent to the north—Dave Hatcher's signal for "note in the bottle under the sink for Stockdale." Like an old fighter pilot, I checked my six o'clock, scooped the note up fast, and concealed it in my prison pajama pants, carefully. Back in my cell, after the guard locked the door, I sat on my toilet bucket—where I could stealthily jettison the note if the peephole cover moved—and unfolded Hatcher's sheet of low-grade paper toweling on which, with a rat dropping, he had printed, without comment or signature, the last verse of Ernest Henley's poem *Invictus*:

> It matters not how strait the gate,
> How charged with punishment the scroll,
> I am the master of my fate:
> I am the captain of my soul.